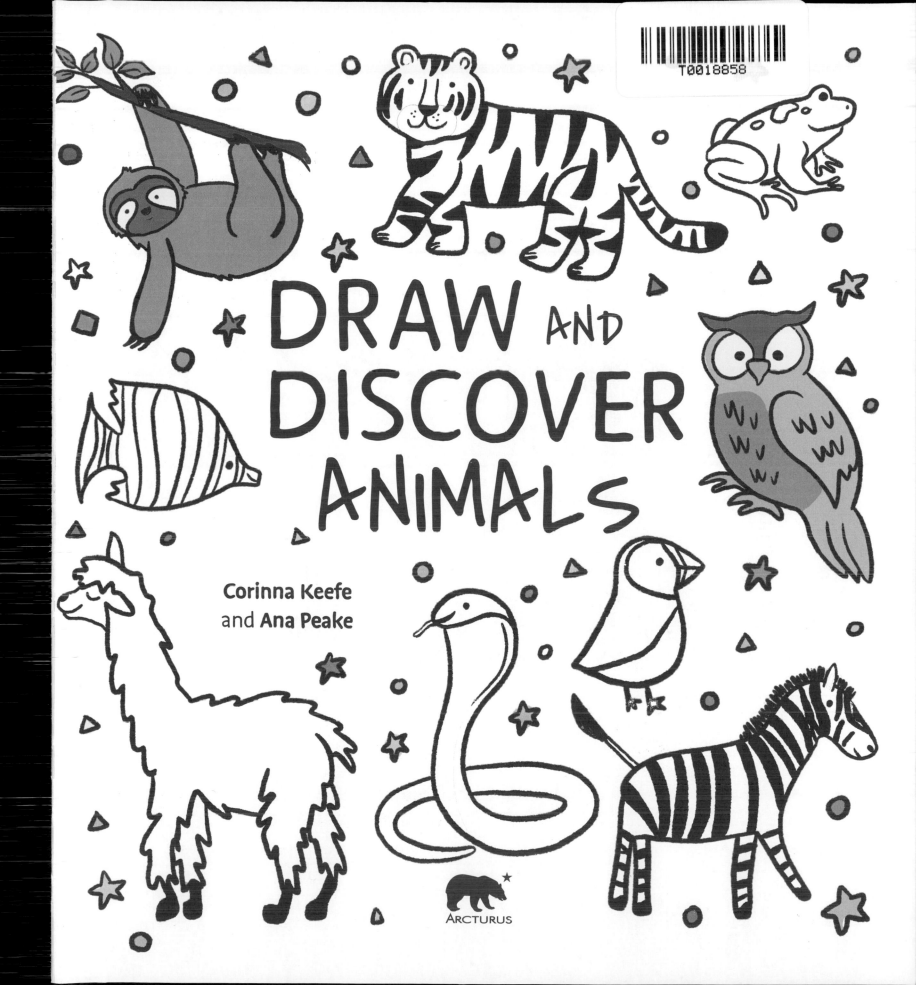

DRAW AND DISCOVER ANIMALS

Corinna Keefe
and Ana Peake

ARCTURUS

ARCTURUS

This edition published in 2024 by Arcturus Publishing Limited,
26/27 Bickels Yard, 151–153 Bermondsey Street, London SE1 3HA

Author: Corinna Keefe
Illustrator: Ana Peake
Editor: Violet Peto
Designer: Stefan Holliland
Managing Editor: Joe Harris

ISBN: 978-1-3988-3683-9
CH011059NT
Supplier 29, Date 1123, PI 00004295

Printed in China

How to Draw ...

How to Draw a Chameleon

1

2

3

4

5

6

7

8

9

Zap!
Chameleons catch food with their long, fast-moving tongues.

Double vision
A chameleon can move its big eyes separately and look in two directions at once.

Up high
Many chameleons like this one live in trees.

All About Chameleons

★ Chameleons change the shade of their skin for communication, camouflage (hiding by looking like the things around you), and to show their emotions.

Steady ...
Its long, curling tail helps the chameleon balance and hold on in the trees.

How to Draw an Owl

1

2

3

4

5

6

7

8

9

Eye spy

Owls have different eyelids for blinking, sleeping, and cleaning their eyes.

What a hoot

They don't just hoot—some can screech, whistle, rattle, hiss, or even bark!

Sneaking around

Owls have special feathers that allow them to hunt prey quietly.

Fancy feet

An owl's feet have toes facing forward and backward!

All About Owls

★ Owls are meat-eaters, meaning that they eat other animals. To find their food, owls rely on their very good eyesight.

★ Unlike humans, owls have tube-shaped eyes! These help them see really far.

How to Draw an Angelfish

1

2

3

4

5

6

7

8

9

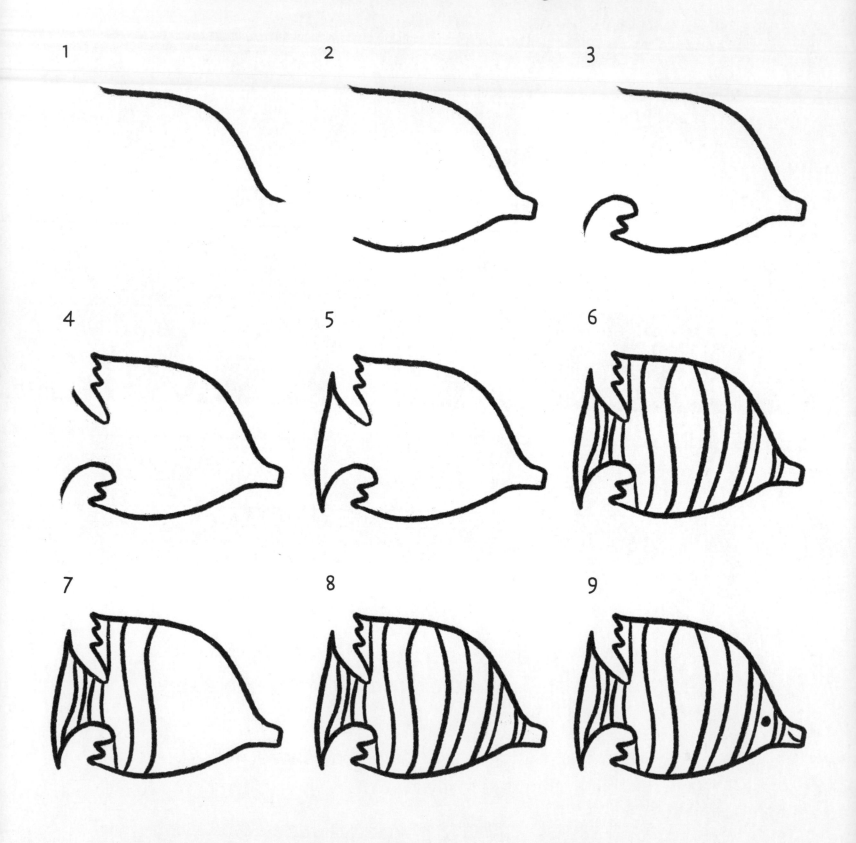

Hide-and-seek

Angelfish have arrow-shaped bodies that help them hide among underwater plants.

Angel bright

Their stripes shine brighter when angelfish are awake, healthy, and happy.

Fantastic fins

Angelfish have long, sail-like fins for steering through the water.

All About Angelfish

★ Baby angelfish have seven black stripes. When they grow up, some of these stripes fade.

★ Pet angelfish are smart enough to remember what time they are fed every day. Don't be late!

How to Draw a Sloth

1

2

3

4

5

6

7

8

9

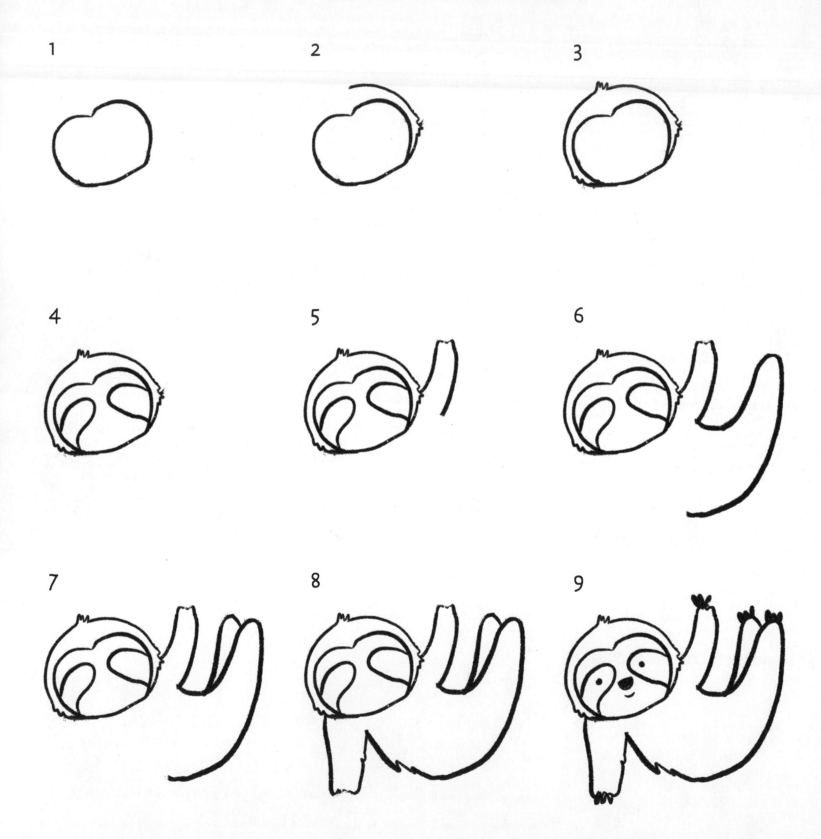

Fur friends

Sloths have green stuff called algae on their fur. This helps them hide. They can also snack on it!

Counting toes

This is a three-toed sloth. It has three long claws on its front and back legs.

Hold on!

Sloths can lock their hands and feet in place to hang upside down for hours!

All About Sloths

* Sloths can sleep for up to 20 hours a day. No wonder the word *sloth* means "laziness!"

How to Draw a Puffin

1

2

3

4

5

6

7

8

9

Beautiful beaks

Puffins are famous for their brightly striped beaks.

Water wings

Puffins' short, strong wings are perfect for "flying" underwater.

All About Puffins

★ Because of their bright beaks, puffins are also called sea parrots or sea clowns!

✱ Puffins live at sea in the colder months. They only land in the spring and summer.

Somewhere safe

Puffins lay their eggs in earth burrows or cracks in the rock.

How to Draw a Cat

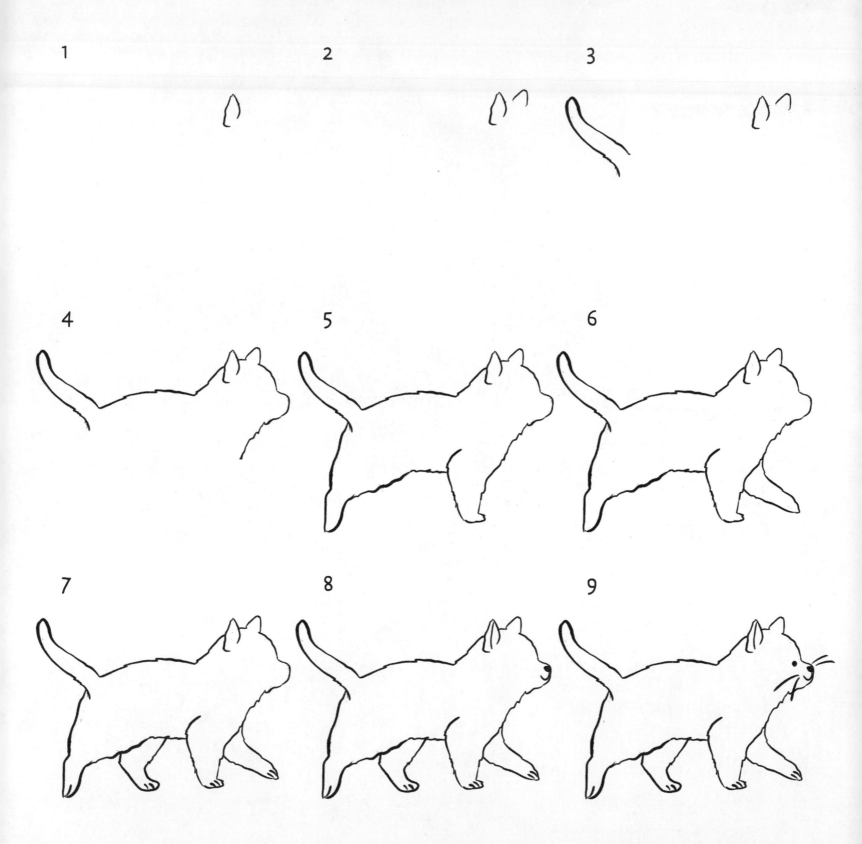

1

2

3

4

5

6

7

8

9

14

All About Cats

* People have been keeping cats as pets for at least 9,500 years.

★ A cat's fur can make up 25 percent of its body weight. That's a lot of fluff!

Fast runners
Cats can run surprisingly quickly when they need to.

Tail talk
Cats use their tails to communicate. Tail up means, "I'm interested!"

Shhh ...
Cats walk on their tiptoes, so that they can move fast and silently.

How to Draw a Brown Bear

1

2

3

4

5

6

7

8

9

All About Bears

★ Brown bears sleep through the winter. They eat a lot of food before then, so that they won't get hungry until spring.

✳ Brown bears are good at fishing. They catch fish with their paws or dive into the water and chase them!

Sharp ears
This bear can hear twice as well as a human. It can hear better than it can see.

Watch out!
A brown bear has long, sharp claws.

What's for dinner?
Brown bears can eat up to 40 kg (90 lb) of food a day. That's about the weight of eight watermelons!

How to Draw a Pelican

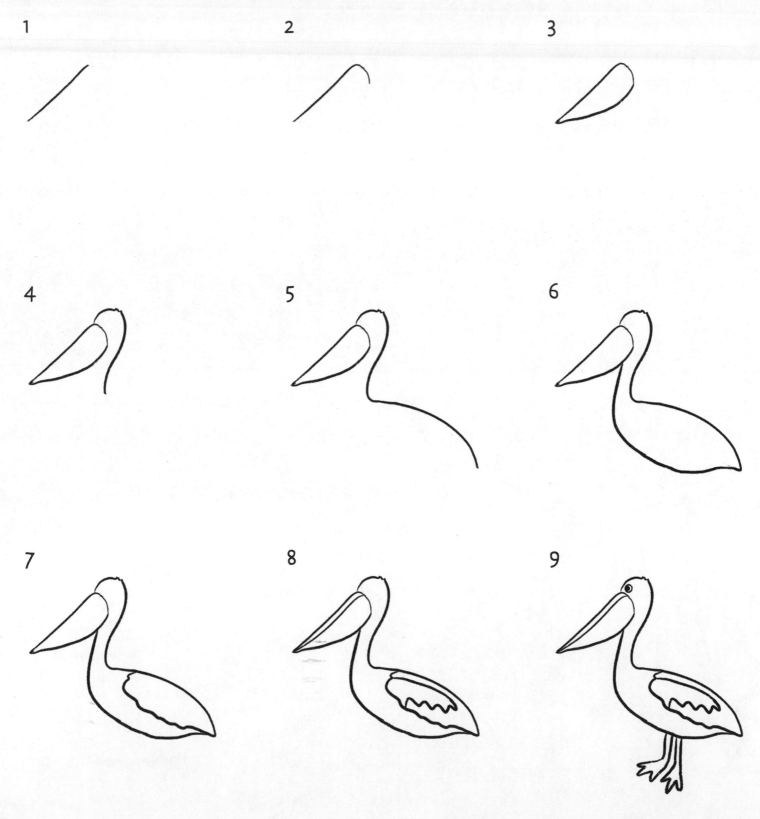

Long bill
Australian pelicans like this have the longest bills of any bird.

What's in the pouch?
Pelicans catch fish by scooping them into a pouch in the lower part of their bill.

Water wader
A pelican's big, webbed feet help it walk through shallow water.

All About Pelicans
* The oldest pelican fossil ever found is from 30 million years ago.

How to Draw a Shark

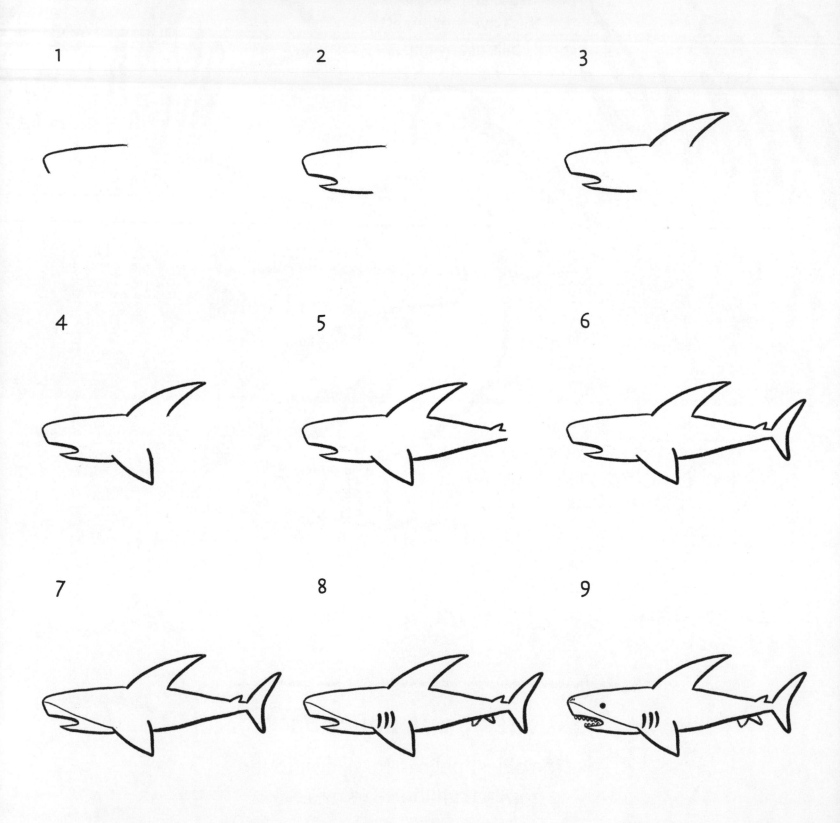

1

2

3

4

5

6

7

8

9

Super senses

A shark has sensors on its head. It uses them to find its way and its food.

What kind of shark?

Blue sharks like this one have a slim body and extra-long front fins.

Night sight

Sharks have a special layer in their eyes that helps them see in the dark.

All About Sharks

★ 97 percent of shark species don't hurt humans ... even if they look a little bit scary!

★ You can put a shark in a trance by flipping it on its back. Scientists use this trick when they want to look at a shark more closely.

How to Draw a Deer

1

2

3

4

5

6

7

8

9

Amazing antlers

Each year, male deer grow antlers in the spring and shed them at the end of winter.

Warm coat

This red deer has thick fur so it can stay warm through the cold months.

All About Deer

★ Deer have four stomachs to help them break down the plants they eat.

✳ Female red deer are called hinds. Male red deer are called stags or harts.

Counting toes

Deer have cloven hooves, with two toes on each hoof.

23

How to Draw a Kiwi

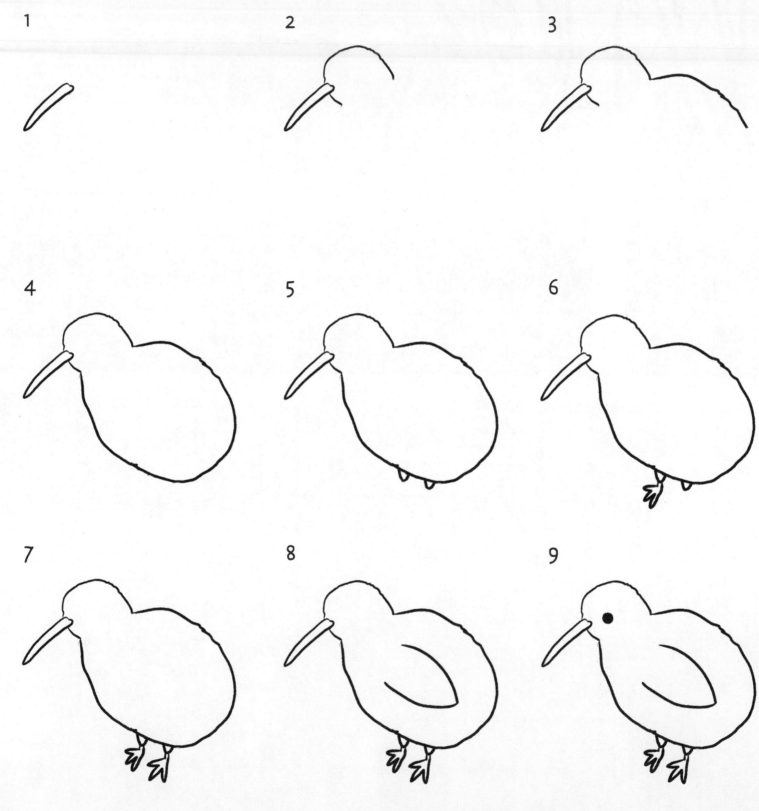

Awesome beaks

Kiwis can't see very well. They use their beaks to sense food using smell and vibrations.

Enormous eggs

Kiwi eggs are very big ... up to 20 percent of the weight of an adult kiwi!

Fluffy feathers

Kiwis use their feathers to stay warm, instead of using them for flying.

All About Kiwis

* Kiwis are the national animal of New Zealand. That's why people from New Zealand are sometimes called Kiwis!

* Baby kiwis have soft, pink beaks when they are born.

How to Draw a Frog

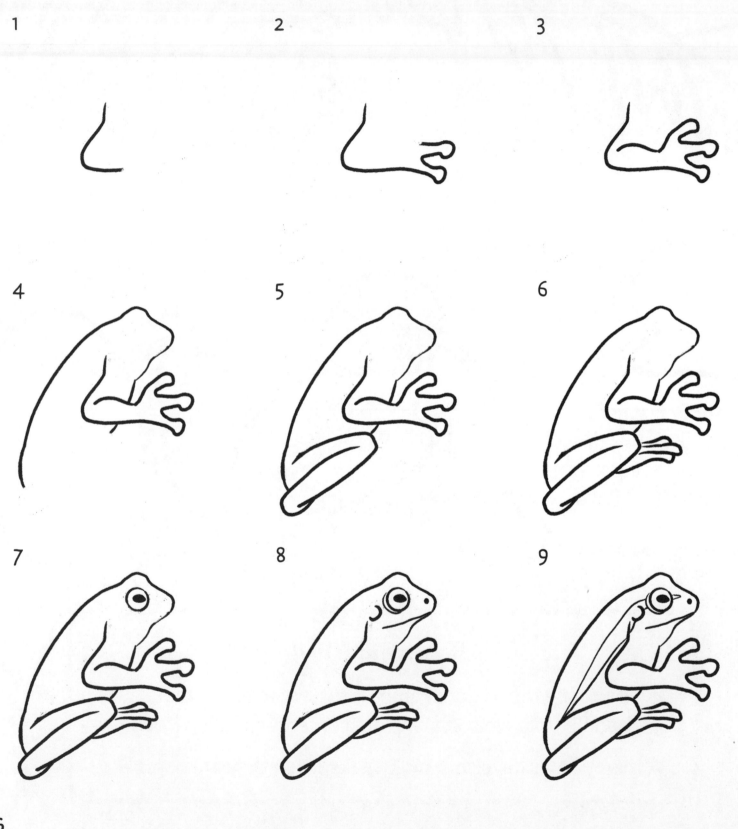

1

2

3

4

5

6

7

8

9

Skin

Tree frogs like this one can be green, brown, or yellow, depending on where they are.

Big eyes

Frogs have big, round eyes that can see all around them. They can also see clearly underwater!

Flying feet

Its big back legs and flat toes help the frog to jump and climb.

All About Frogs

★ Tree frogs croak when it's about to rain.

✳ There are tree frogs on every continent in the world ... except Antarctica!

How to Draw a Zebra

1

2

3

4

5

6

7

8

9

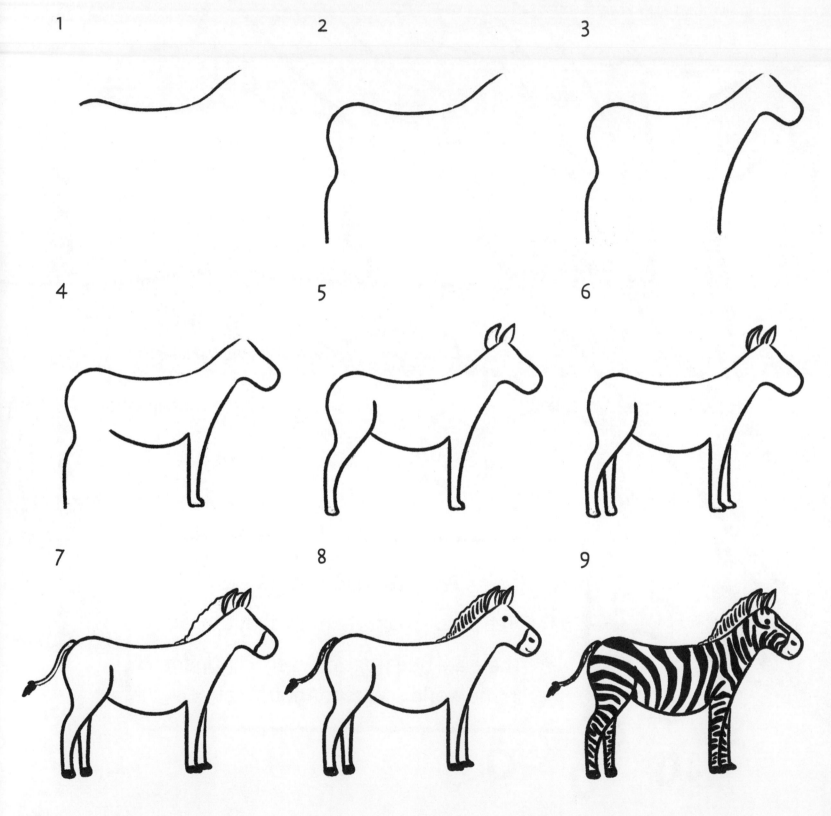

All About Zebras

* Zebras usually hang out in large herds of up to 1,000 animals.

★ Zebras use their strong back legs to kick when they feel they are in danger.

Black and white
Every zebra has a unique pattern of stripes.

Listen up
Zebras use their big ears to listen for danger.

Shoo!
Zebras use their tufted tails to keep flies away.

How to Draw a Squirrel

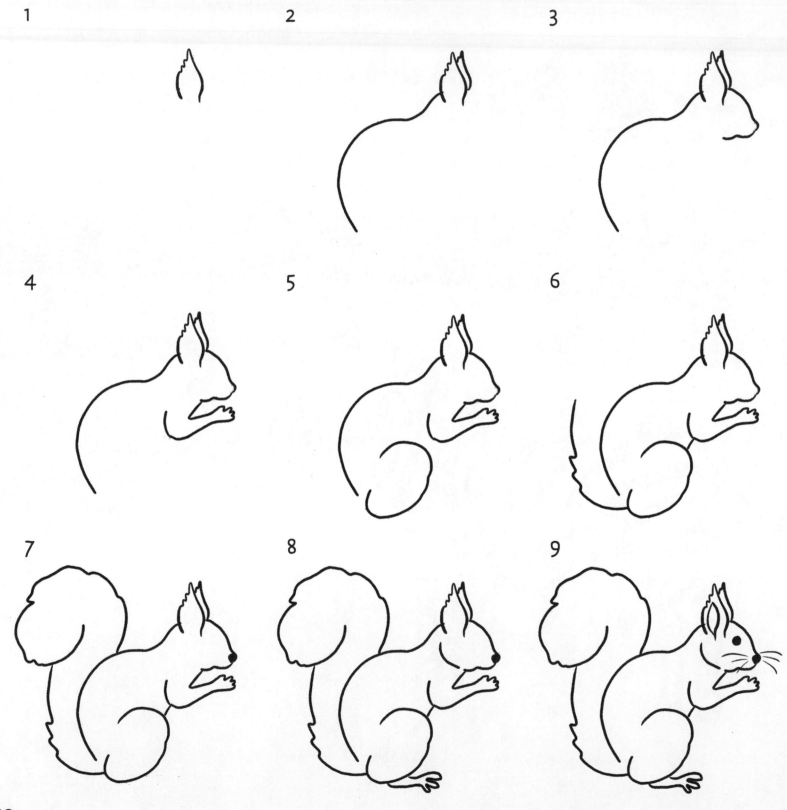

1

2

3

4

5

6

7

8

9

All About Squirrels

★ Squirrels are really good at collecting and storing food.

✴ They have special pouches in their cheeks for holding nuts, seeds, and berries.

Tall tails

Squirrels use their bushy tails to balance, for shelter, and to signal to other squirrels.

Nutty nibblers

They have strong front teeth so that they can bite tough nuts and seeds.

Wow!

Squirrels can point their feet backward to run down trees head first!

How to Draw an Octopus

1

2

3

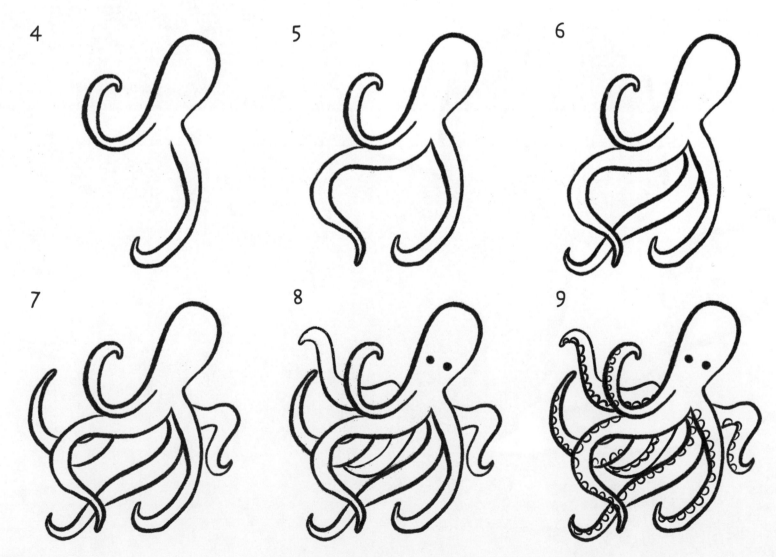

4

5

6

7

8

9

32

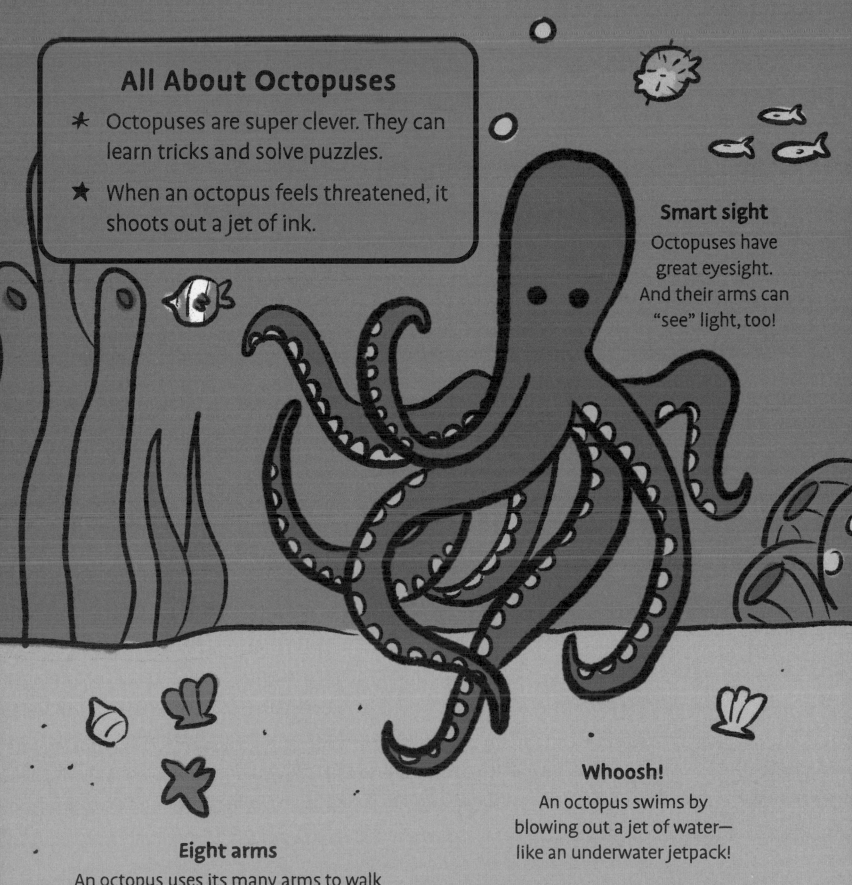

All About Octopuses

* Octopuses are super clever. They can learn tricks and solve puzzles.

* When an octopus feels threatened, it shoots out a jet of ink.

Smart sight
Octopuses have great eyesight. And their arms can "see" light, too!

Eight arms
An octopus uses its many arms to walk on the seafloor and look for food.

Whoosh!
An octopus swims by blowing out a jet of water— like an underwater jetpack!

How to Draw a Crocodile

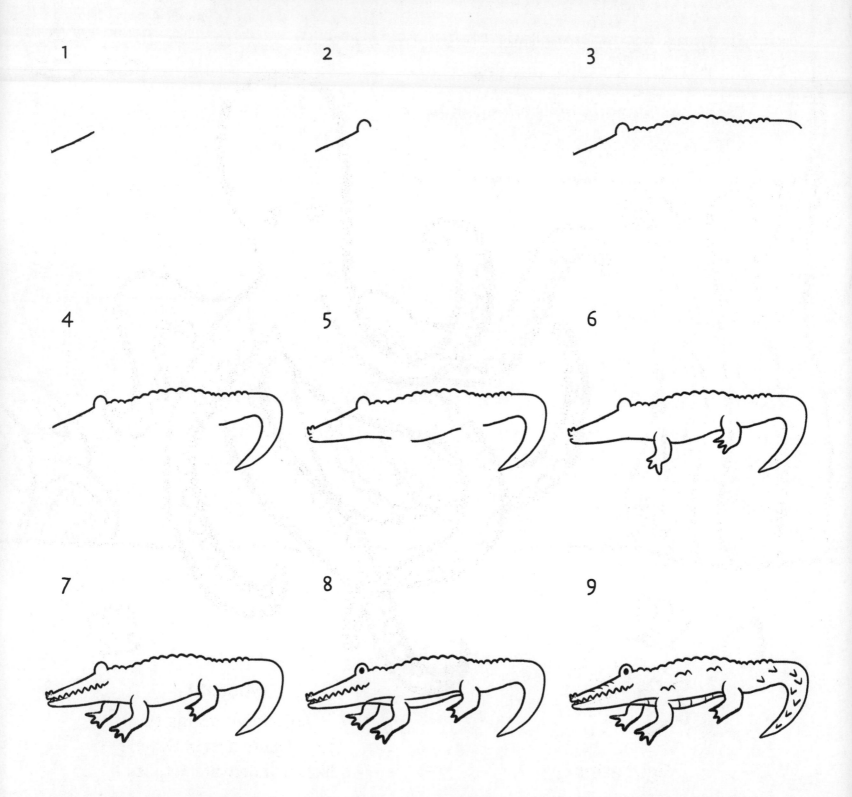

All About Crocodiles

★ Crocodiles are cold-blooded. When they get too cold in the water, they have to come on shore to sunbathe.

✳ Crocodiles have been roaming the Earth for about 240 million years.

How many teeth?

Crocodiles have 80 teeth. They can regrow them up to 50 times.

Sneaky senses

A crocodile's eyes are on top of its head, so it can lurk in the water but still see what's going on.

Swimming skills

Crocodiles use their webbed feet to turn quickly in the water.

How to Draw a Turkey

1

2

3

4

5

6

7

8

9

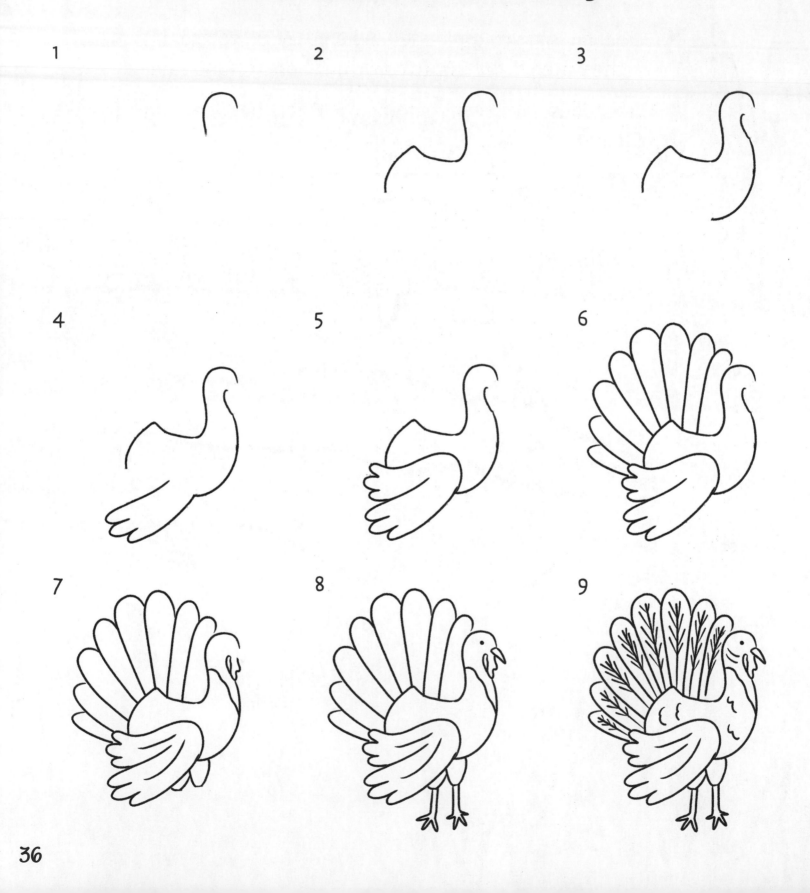

Bird's-eye view
Turkeys can see three
times better than
humans!

Wattle what?
The big red wattle
(flap of skin) around a
turkey's beak is called
a snood.

Rainbow bird
A turkey's head can be red,
blue, or white, depending on
its mood!

All About Turkeys

* Turkeys spend most of
  their time on the ground
  —but in the wild, they
  sleep in trees.

* Male turkeys use their
  fancy feathers to show
  off to each other.

How to Draw a Gecko

1

2

3

4

5

6

7

8

9

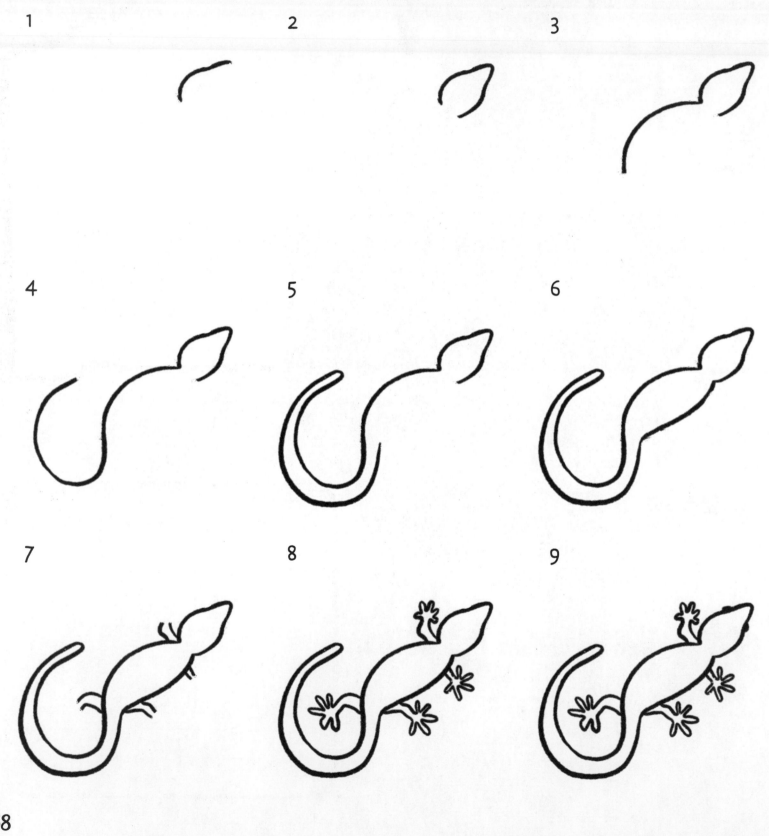

Slurp!

Geckos don't blink. They have a special clear covering on their eyeballs and lick them to keep them clean.

All About Geckos

★ Geckos can change the pattern of their skin for camouflage.

✳ Most geckos come out at night. They are able to see well in low light.

Superpowers

Geckos can climb anywhere because of tiny, sticky hairs on their feet.

Trick tail

Geckos can shed their tails if they need to get away from a predator fast.

How to Draw a Wolf

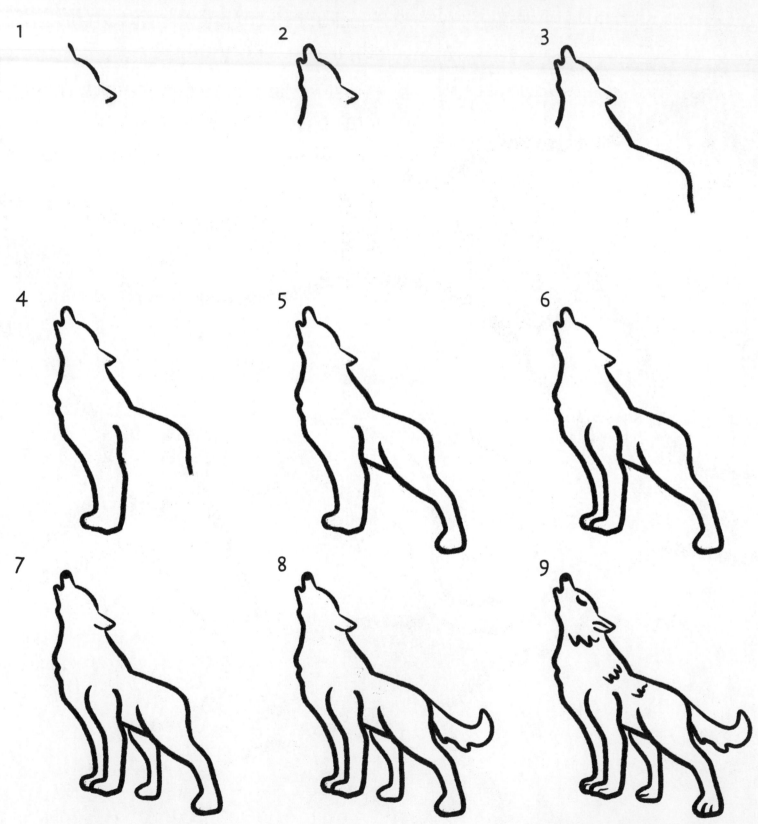

1

2

3

4

5

6

7

8

9

Awoooooo!

Howling is how wolves talk to each other over long distances.

All About Wolves

* Wolves can hunt large animals because they are good at working together in a pack.

* Wolves can see, smell, and hear even better than dogs. They can smell 100 times better than humans!

Warm wolves

Wolves can live in really cold places because they have thick, fluffy fur.

Long legs

Wolves have long back legs. These help them run fast, even in deep snow.

How to Draw a Gorilla

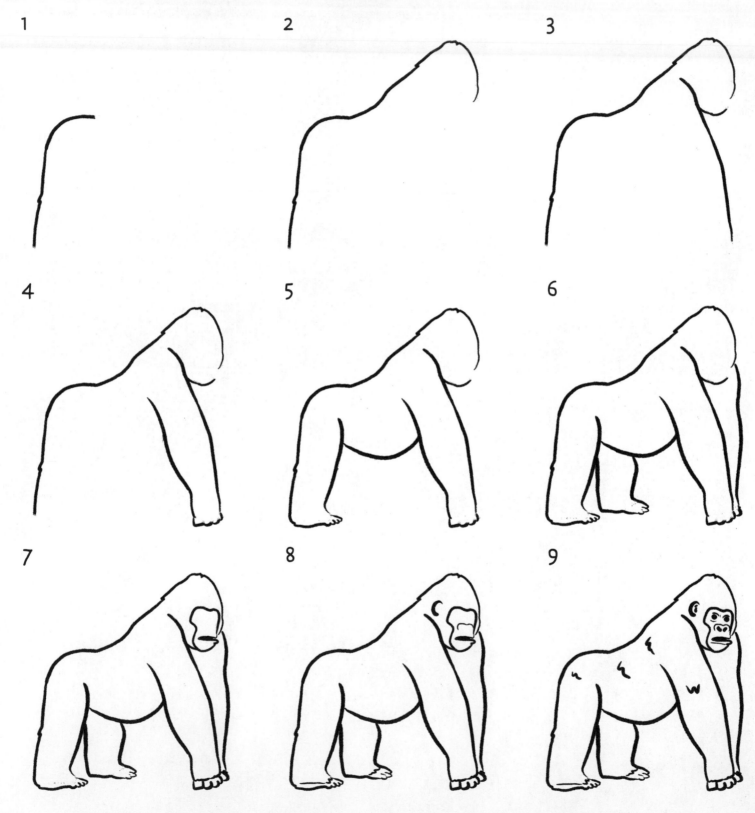

All About Gorillas

★ Gorillas are about the same height as humans, but 10 times stronger.

✳ Gorillas can make tools and even learn basic sign language.

Who's the boss?

The leader of a gorilla troop is called a silverback because he has silver fur on his back.

Funny face

When a gorilla opens its mouth without showing its teeth, that means it wants to play!

On all fours

Gorillas like to walk on their knuckles most of the time.

How to Draw a Seahorse

1

2

3

4

5

6

7

8

9

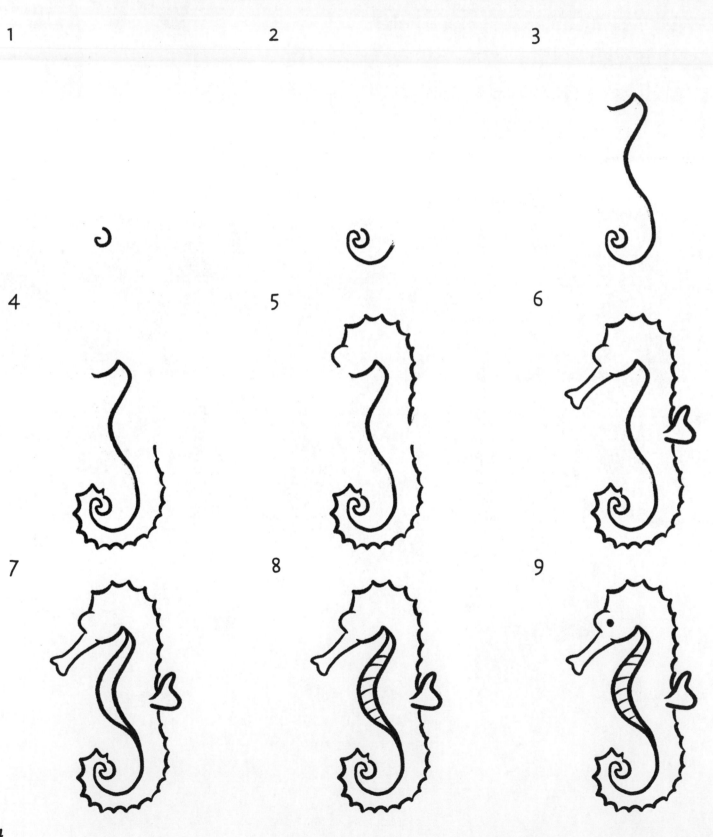

All About Seahorses

* A seahorse steers through the water with its back fin. It moves up and down using an air bubble inside its body!

* After the female seahorse lays eggs, the male keeps them in a special pouch until they hatch.

Sneaky snout

Seahorses use camouflage to hide from their prey. Then they suck it up through their snouts!

Tough skin

Seahorse skin is made of spiny plates to protect it from harm.

Time to rest

Seahorses can use their tails to hold on to coral.

How to Draw a Polar Bear

1

2

3

4

5

6

7

8

9

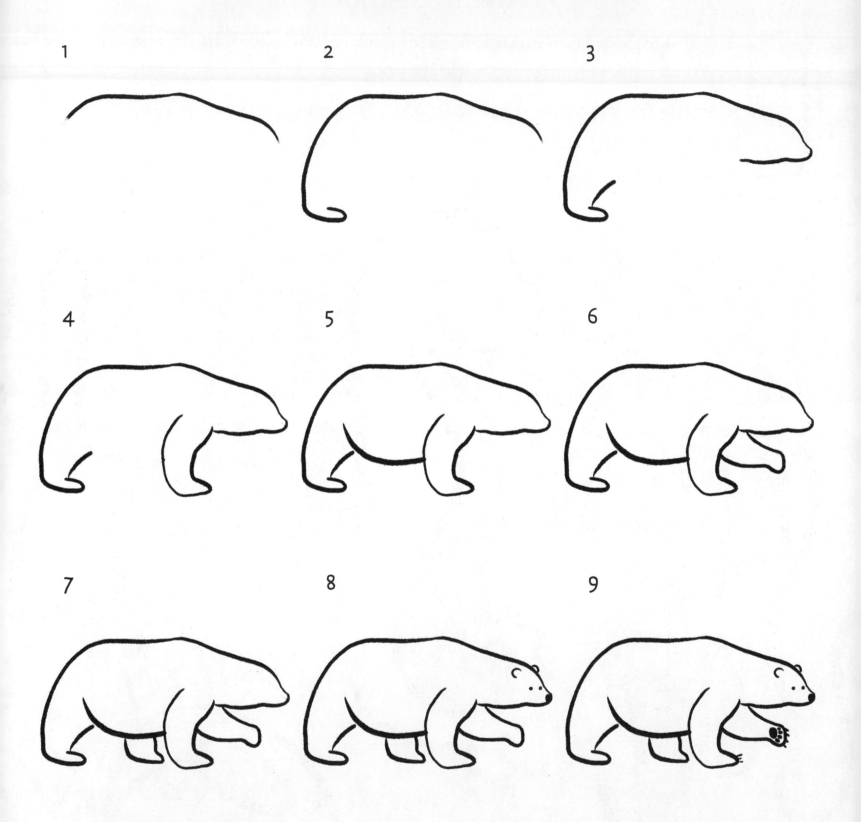

Big bears

A polar bear can be more than 2.5 m (8 ft) tall standing upright—about the height of a doorframe.

All About Polar Bears

★ A polar bear's skin is black under its white fur. The fur is for camouflage, while its black skin is for warmth.

✳ Polar bears are strong swimmers! They use their giant front paws to paddle through the water.

Super smell

Polar bears can smell animals up to 1.6 km (1 mile) away.

Extra grip

The pads on the bear's paws are covered in bumps to help it grip the ice.

How to Draw a Bat

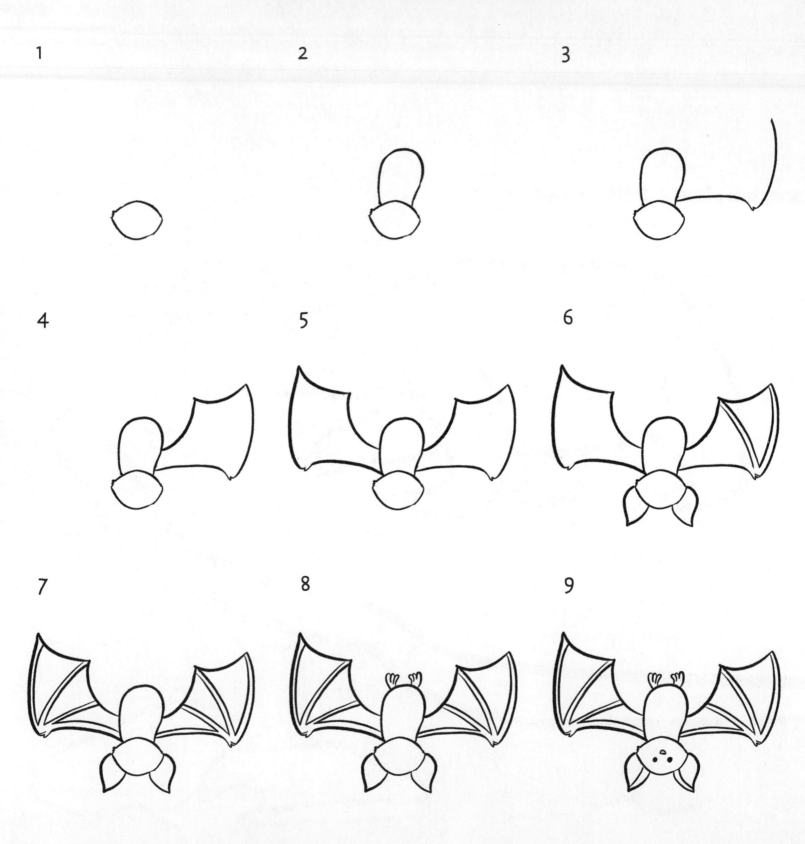

1

2

3

4

5

6

7

8

9

48

Fabulous fliers

Bats are the only mammals that can fly.

Upside down

Bats sleep like this so that if a predator attacks, they can fly off right away.

Blind as a bat

Instead of their eyes, bats use their hearing to "see" the world.

Wings or hands?

Bat wings are like very thin, webbed hands, with four long fingers and a thumb.

All About Bats

* There are over 1,300 different bat species. That's a fifth of all the mammals on Earth!

★ When it's flying, a bat's heart will beat up to 1,000 times a minute.

How to Draw a Rhino

1

2

3

4

5

6

7

8

9

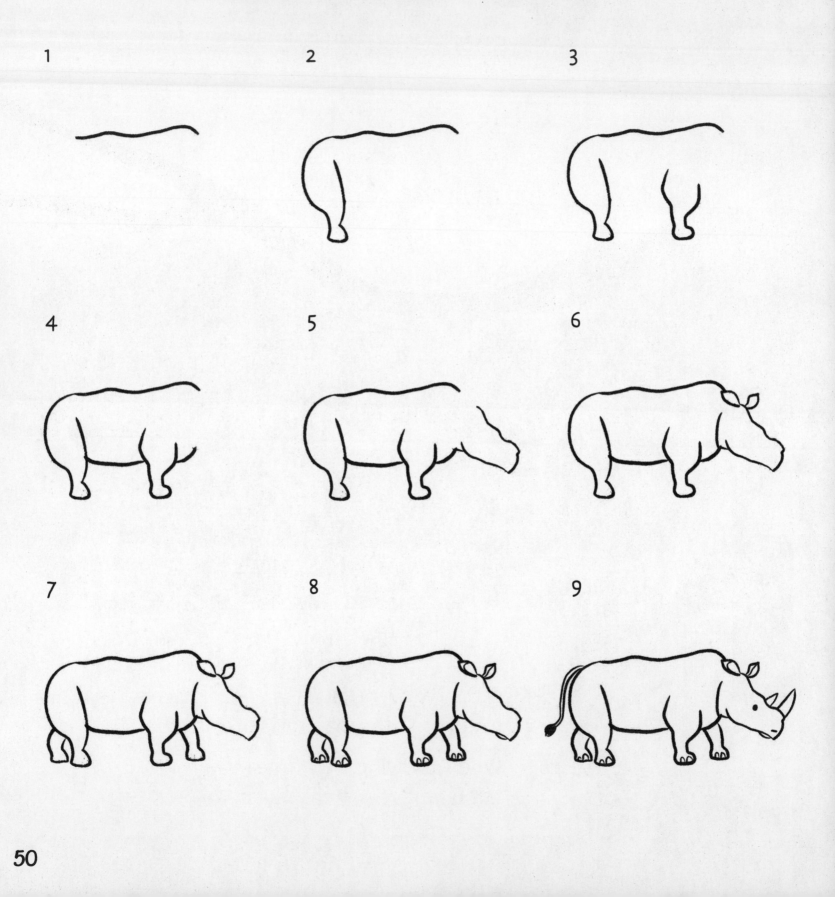

Ancient animals

Rhinos have been around for millions of years.

Best friends

Oxpecker birds like to ride on rhinos. They eat bugs to keep the rhino's skin clean.

How many horns?

African rhinos like this have two horns. Other types have just one.

Keen ears

Rhinos can smell and hear very well.

All About Rhinos

★ Some rhinos live in groups called crashes!

✳ Rhinos love wallowing in mud. It's like natural sunscreen and helps protect them from insect bites.

How to Draw a Hedgehog

1

2

3

4

5

6

7

8

9

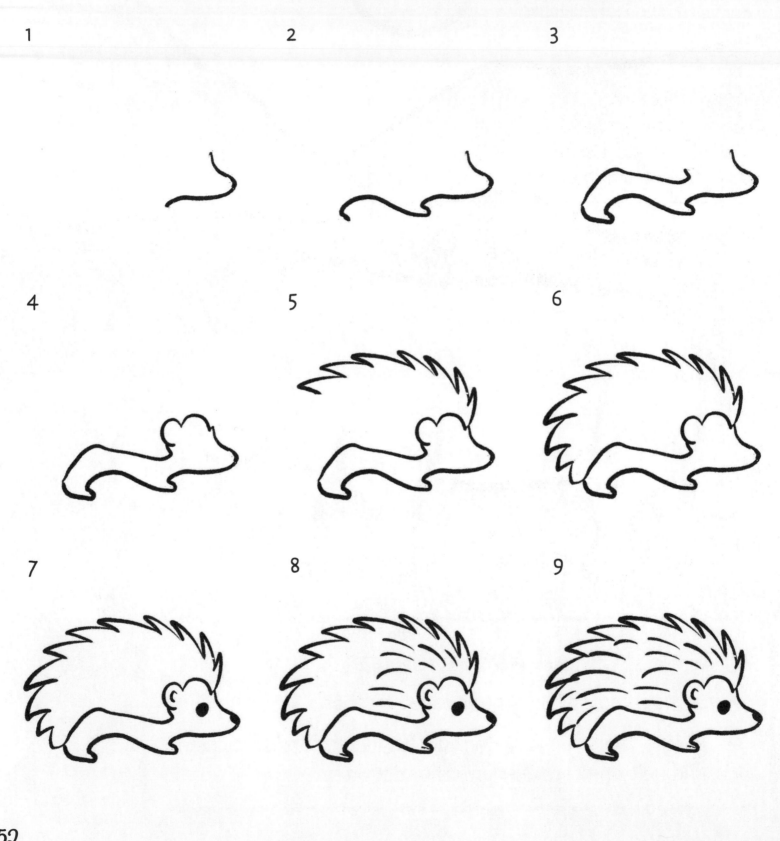

Stay back!

Hedgehogs have 5,000 spines that protect them from other animals.

Snuffle snuffle

They have a good sense of hearing and smell, even though they can't see very well.

Yum!

Hedgehogs like to eat beetles, worms, slugs, and snails.

All About Hedgehogs

* Hedgehogs are active at night. During the day, they curl up in a nest of leaves, moss, and grass.

How to Draw a Tiger

1

2

3

4

5

6

7

8

9

Big cats

Tigers are the biggest members of the cat family.

Special stripes

Every tiger has a different pattern of stripes. These help to camouflage them.

All About Tigers

★ A tiger's roar can be heard from up to 3 km (1.8 miles) away.

✳ Tiger pee smells like buttered popcorn!

Steady ...

Tigers use their tails to balance when they're moving fast.

How to Draw a Dolphin

Snap!
Dolphins have sharp, cone-shaped teeth for catching food.

Who nose?
This kind of dolphin is called a bottlenose dolphin.

All About Dolphins

* Dolphins live in groups, or pods, of about 12 dolphins.

★ They use squeaks, whistles, and clicks to communicate with each other.

Up, up, and away!
Dolphins can leap about 9 m (30 ft)—that's the height of a three-floor building!

Splash!
They use their strong tails to power through the water.

How to Draw a Koala

1

2

3

4

5

6

7

8

9

Yum!
Koalas mainly munch
on eucalyptus leaves.

Sniff, sniff ...
Koalas use their big
noses to sniff out the
juiciest leaves.

**Warm
and fuzzy**
Koala fur is
thick and
warm—ready
for all
weathers!

All About Koalas

★ Eucalyptus leaves
are tough and
poisonous. Koalas
are one of the only
animals that can
eat them.

✳ Koalas can sleep for
up to 18 hours a day!

Hold on!
A koala's strong,
curved claws help it
climb trees.

How to Draw an Eagle

1

2

3

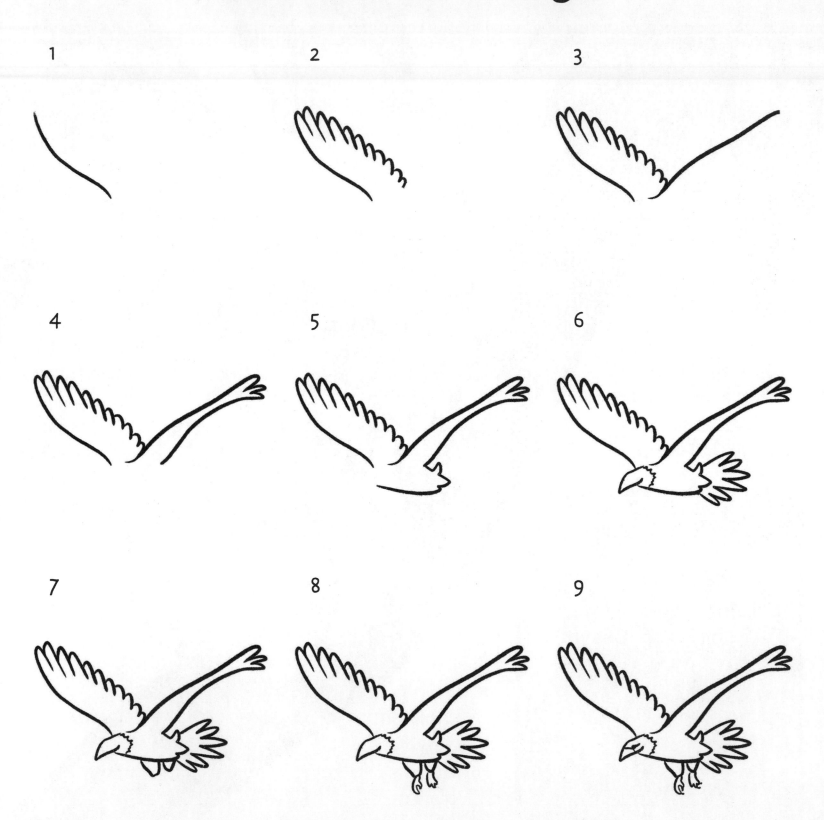

4

5

6

7

8

9

60

Wide wings

Bald eagles have a wingspan of more than 2 m (6.6 ft)—the height of a really tall person.

That's sharp!

The eagle uses its razor-sharp claws to catch and hold prey.

Out of sight!

Eagles have amazing eyesight. They can spot prey from 1.6 km (1 mile) away.

All About Eagles

* Bald eagles like this one are a kind of sea eagle. They eat mainly fish.

★ Bald eagles aren't really bald. Their name comes from an old English word, *balde*, which means white!

How to Draw a Snake

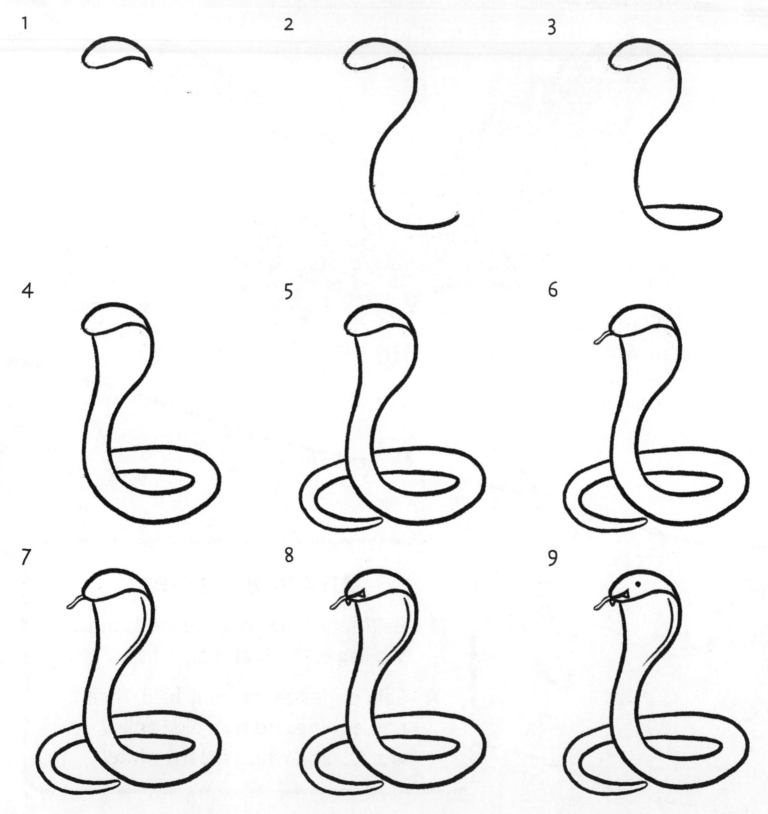

All About Cobras

★ King cobras can make a sound just like a dog growling.

✳ A single cobra bite has enough venom to kill an elephant.

Monster mouth

A cobra's fangs are packed with venom, which it uses to kill its prey.

Puffed up

A cobra puffs out the hood around its neck to scare off predators.

Hungry snakes

King cobras eat other snakes and their eggs, as well as lizards, birds, rats, and mice.

Scaly skin

The snake's scales help it move smoothly over all kinds of surfaces.

How to Draw a Giraffe

1

2

3

4

5

6

7

8

9

Stre-e-e-e-etch!
Giraffes use their long necks to eat leaves from tall trees.

All About Giraffes

* Giraffes are the tallest land animal. They can grow up to 5.5 m (18 ft) tall—a bit taller than the height of a basketball hoop.

* They have long, purple-black tongues.

Camo coats
Each giraffe has a unique pattern on its coat for camouflage.

How to Draw a Rabbit

1

2

3

4

5

6

7

8

9

Wow!
Rabbits can turn their ears around to figure out exactly where a sound is coming from.

Bunny hop
Rabbits have strong back legs that help them jump really high!

All About Rabbits

★ Baby rabbits are called kits or kittens ... just like cats!

✳ Rabbits dig underground homes called warrens.

Turn tail
Rabbit tails are white so that when they run away, other rabbits notice and run away, too!

How to Draw a Clownfish

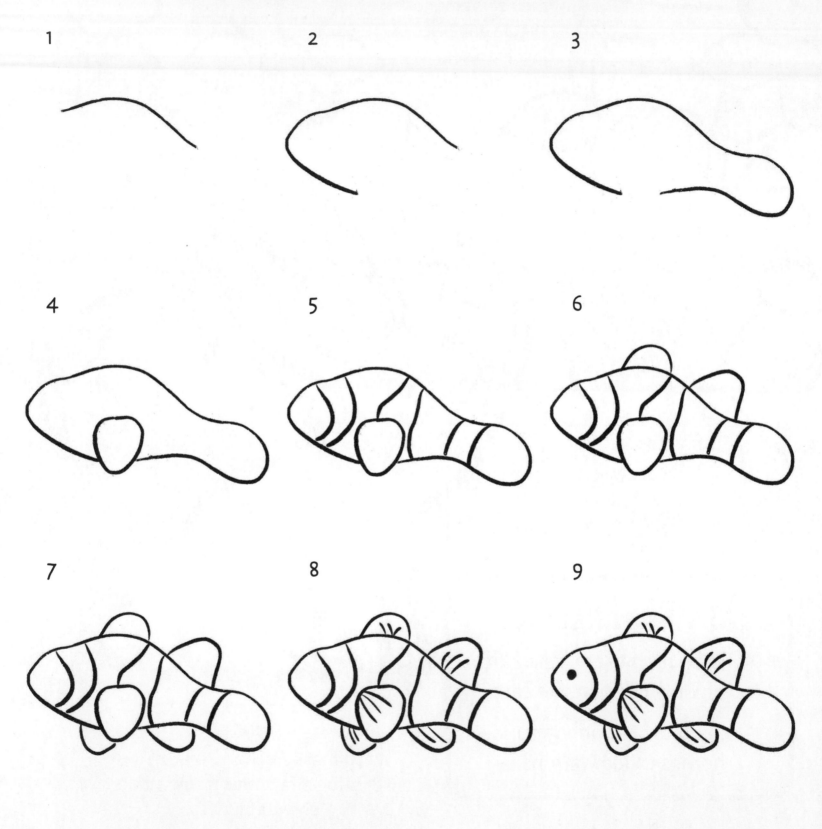

1

2

3

4

5

6

7

8

9

68

A happy pairing

Clownfish live among the stinging tentacles of sea anemones. These protect the fish. In return, clownfish provide food scraps for the anemones.

Male or female?

All clownfish are born male. Later, they can switch and become female.

Cute clowns

Clownfish are very small—about the size of a teacup!

All About Clownfish

* Clownfish talk to each other with popping and clicking noises!

★ A layer of slimy stuff called mucus on the clownfish's scales protects it from anemone stings.

How to Draw a Raccoon

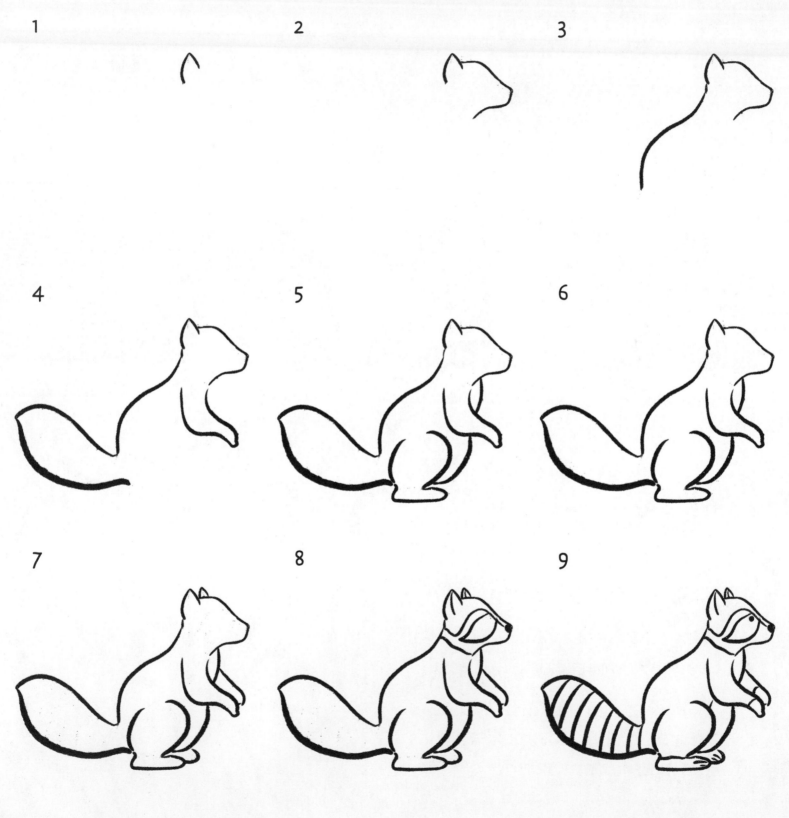

All About Raccoons

★ Raccoons are good climbers, swimmers, and fishers.

✳ They have sensitive front paws, which they use to handle objects. They can even unlace shoes!

Mischief-makers

Raccoons look like they are wearing masks ... like bandits!

Nightlife

Raccoons mostly come out at night.

Fuzzy fur

A raccoon's fur helps it stay warm in cold weather.

How to Draw a Flamingo

1

2

3

4

5

6

7

8

9

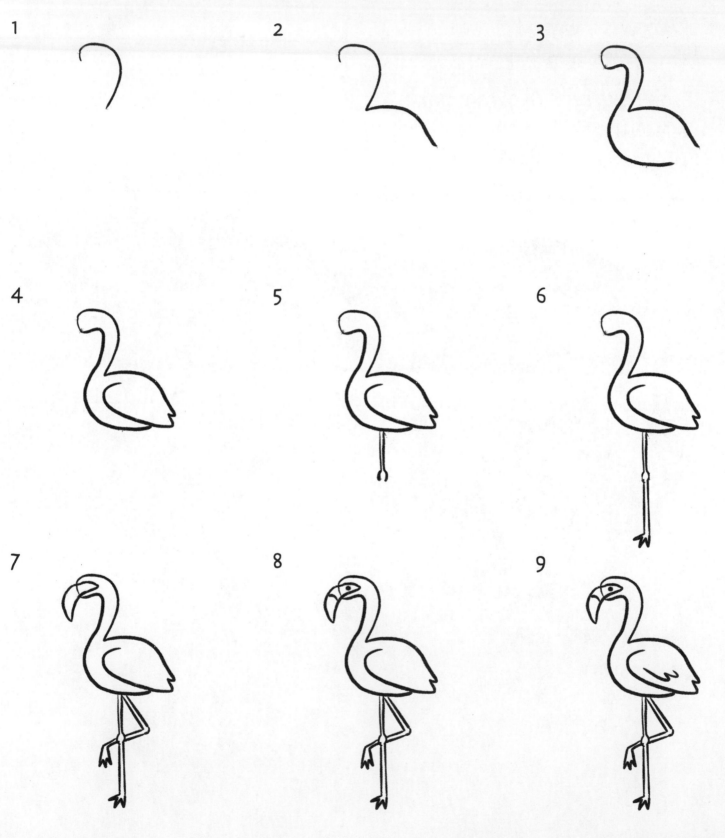

Flaming pink
Adult flamingos range from pink to red, depending on what they eat.

Dinner time
To catch food, flamingos scoop their heads through the water ... upside down!

Steady ...
Flamingos like to stand on one leg. They're comfortable that way!

All About Flamingos
* Baby flamingos are white. They turn pink when they're two years old.

* At certain times, huge groups of flamingos will dance to impress each other.

How to Draw a Crab

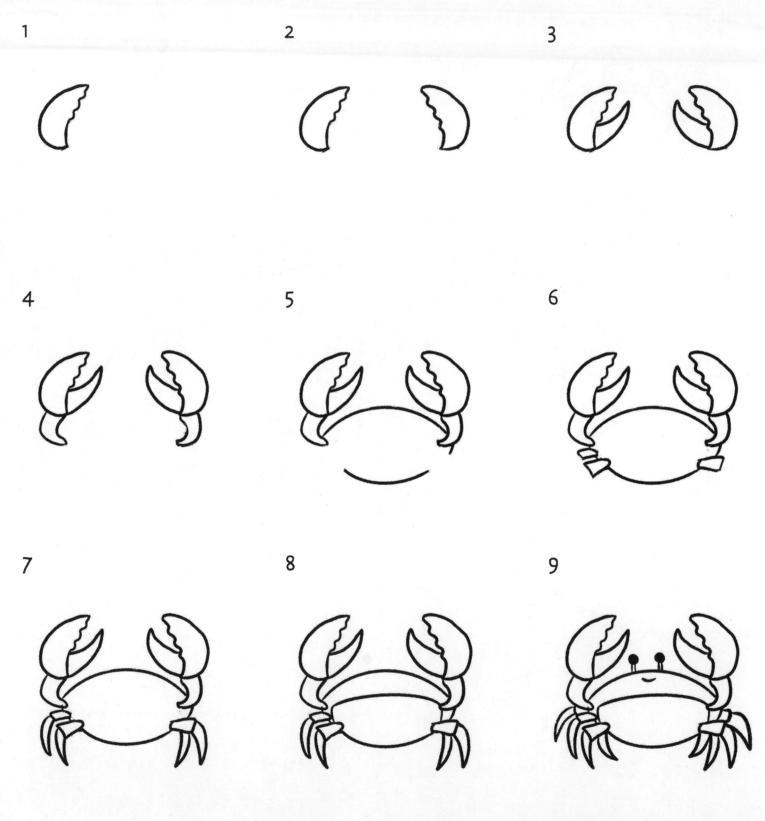

1

2

3

4

5

6

7

8

9

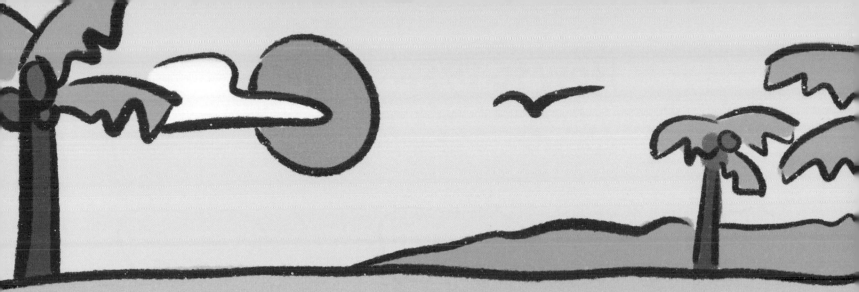

Crab's-eye view

A crab's eyes are on stalks so it can see more.

How many?

Crabs have 10 legs, including their front claws.

Side shuffle

Crabs can walk in any direction ... but they prefer to move sideways.

All About Crabs

★ There are over 4,500 different crab types.

✳ Some types of crabs can shed their claws and grow new ones.

How to Draw a Horse

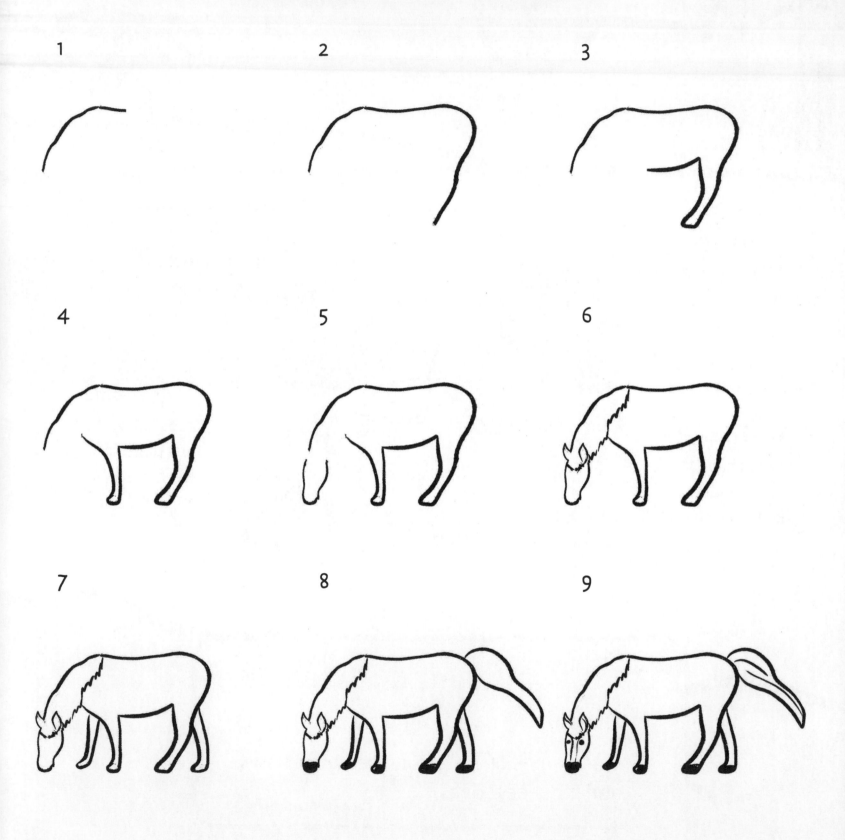

1

2

3

4

5

6

7

8

9

All About Horses

* There are around 60 million horses in the world today.

* Humans have been using horses for thousands of years.

Enormous eyes

Horses have bigger eyes than any other land mammal— and three eyelids!

Deep breath!

Horses can only breathe through their noses, not their mouths.

Super sleep

Horses can lock their legs in place and go to sleep standing up.

How to Draw an Ostrich

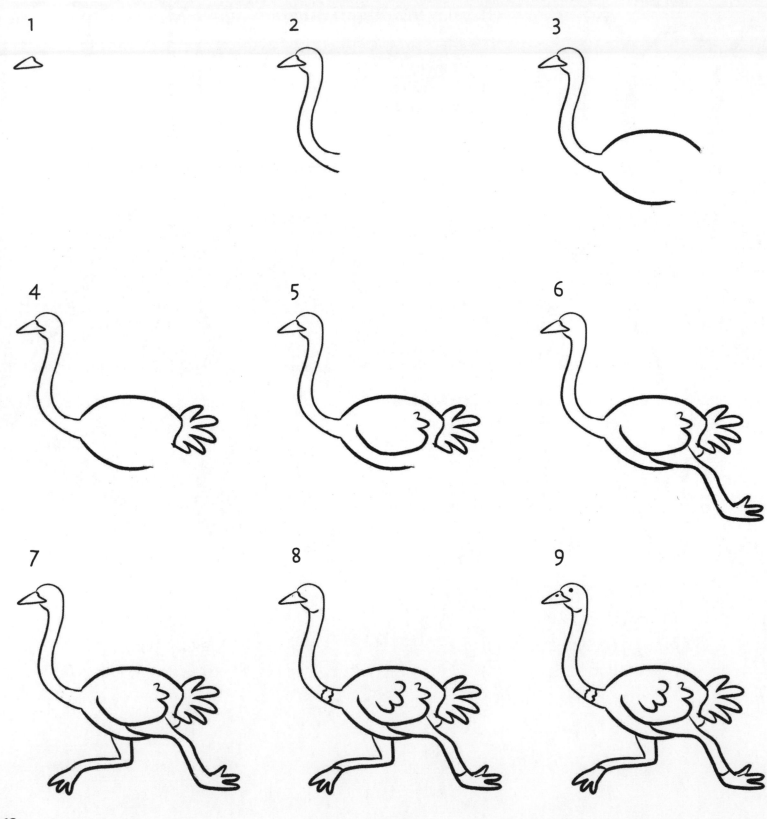

All About Ostriches

★ Ostriches don't just use their legs for running. They can also kick when they feel threatened.

✳ Ostriches lay the largest eggs in the world—about 24 times the size of a hen's egg!

Fast feathers
Ostriches can't fly ... but they can run really fast.

Biggest bird
Ostriches are the world's largest bird. They can be up to 2.7 m (9 ft) tall—taller than a giraffe!

Snappy dressers
Male ostriches like this one have black and white feathers. Females are brown.

How to Draw a Platypus

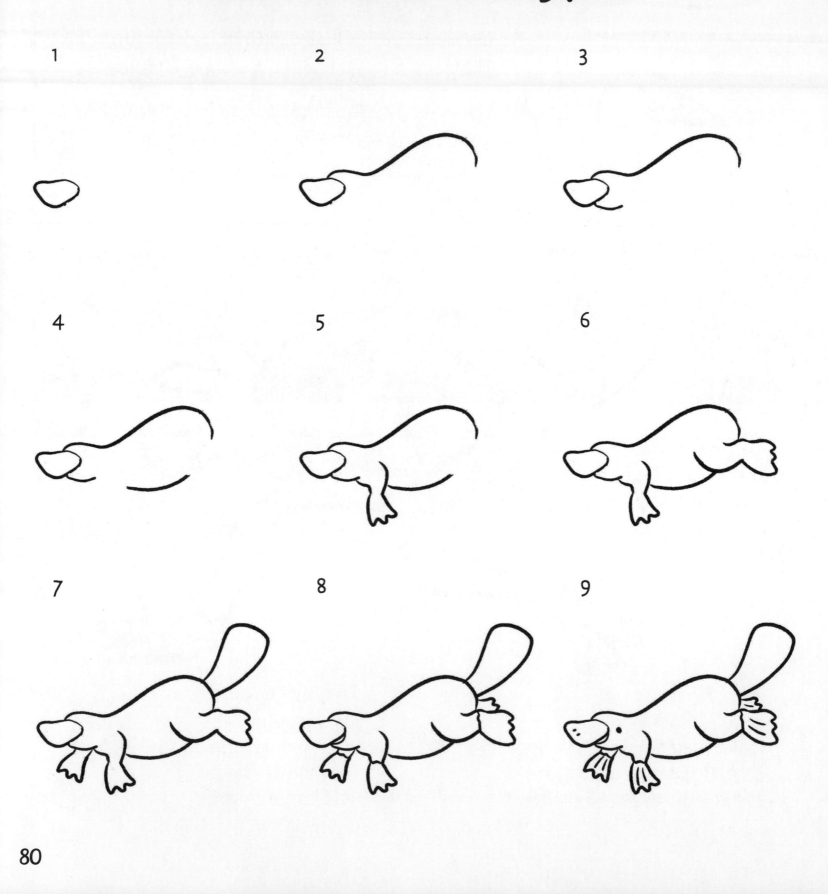

1

2

3

4

5

6

7

8

9

All About Platypuses

* Platypuses are one of just two types of mammals that lay eggs.

★ They have two layers of fur for extra warmth and waterproofing.

Smart snout
Platypuses can detect signals with their bills—like sharks!

Spiky surprise!
A platypus has a venomous spur or point on its hind feet.

Tail tiller
They use their wide, flat tails to steer through the water.

How to Draw an Alpaca

1

2

3

4

5

6

7

8

9

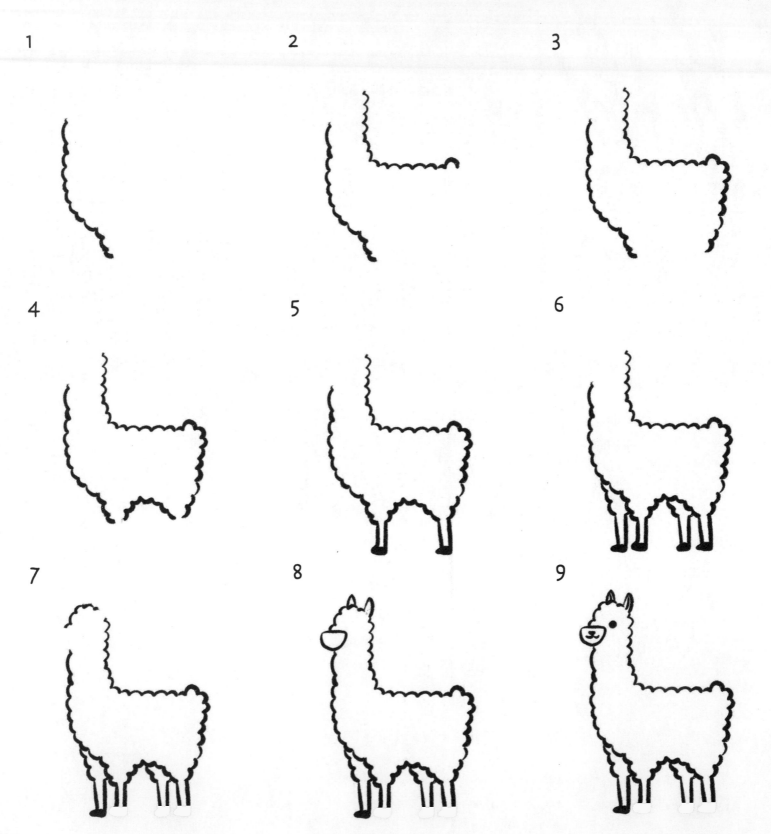

82

All About Alpacas

★ Alpacas look similar to llamas, which are larger and stronger.

✳ Humans have been farming alpacas for at least 6,000 years.

Spitting mad

When alpacas get angry, they spit!

Soft as clouds

Alpacas have warm, soft wool that is perfect for making cloth.

Tough toes

The alpaca has four toes on each hoof. This is useful for walking on stony trails.

How to Draw a Monkey

1

2

3

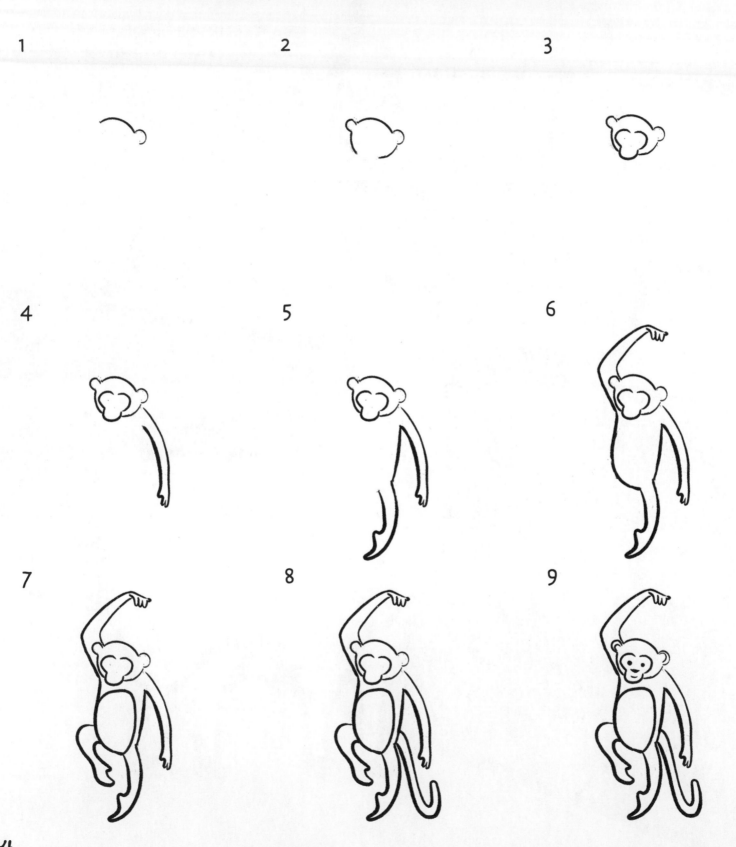

4

5

6

7

8

9

84

That's handy!

Monkeys have fingers and thumbs, like humans do.

Hanging out

Many monkeys, like this one, spend most of their time in the trees.

All About Monkeys

* There are 264 different types of monkeys. That's a lot!

★ The smallest type of monkey is about the size of a banana. The largest is as big as a dog!

Talented tails

Monkeys use their tails to balance and hang from trees.

How to Draw a Turtle

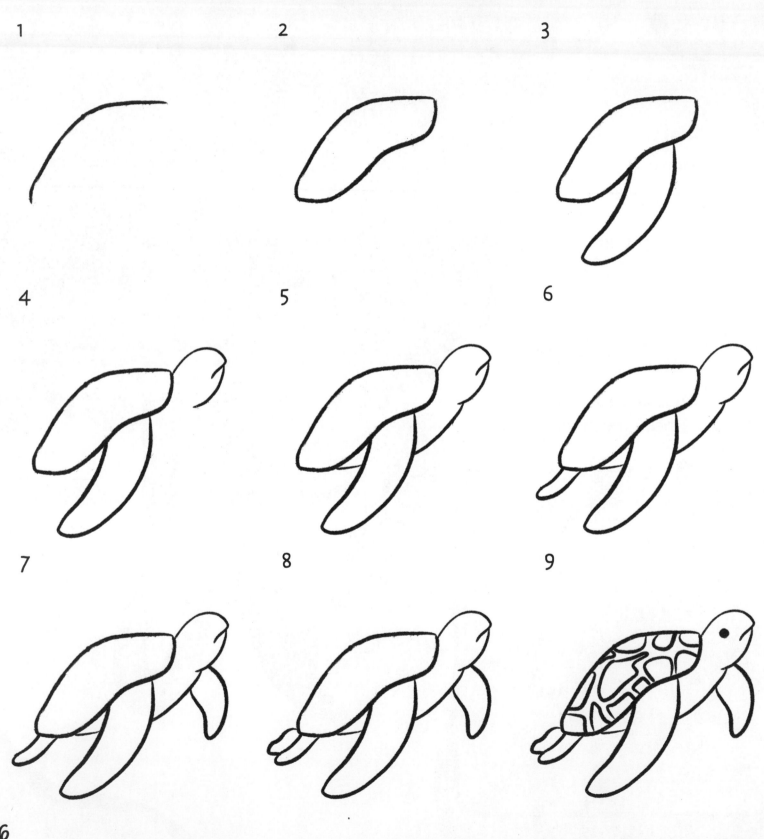

1

2

3

4

5

6

7

8

9

All About Turtles

★ Turtles have been around on Earth for 200 million years.

✳ Even though turtles live at sea, they lay their eggs on land.

Snap!
Turtles have sharp beaks instead of teeth.

Safe shell
The turtle's shell acts as protection. It's really part of its skeleton!

Flip out
Turtles use their giant flippers to steer through the water.

How to Draw a Fox

1

2

3

4

5

6

7

8

9

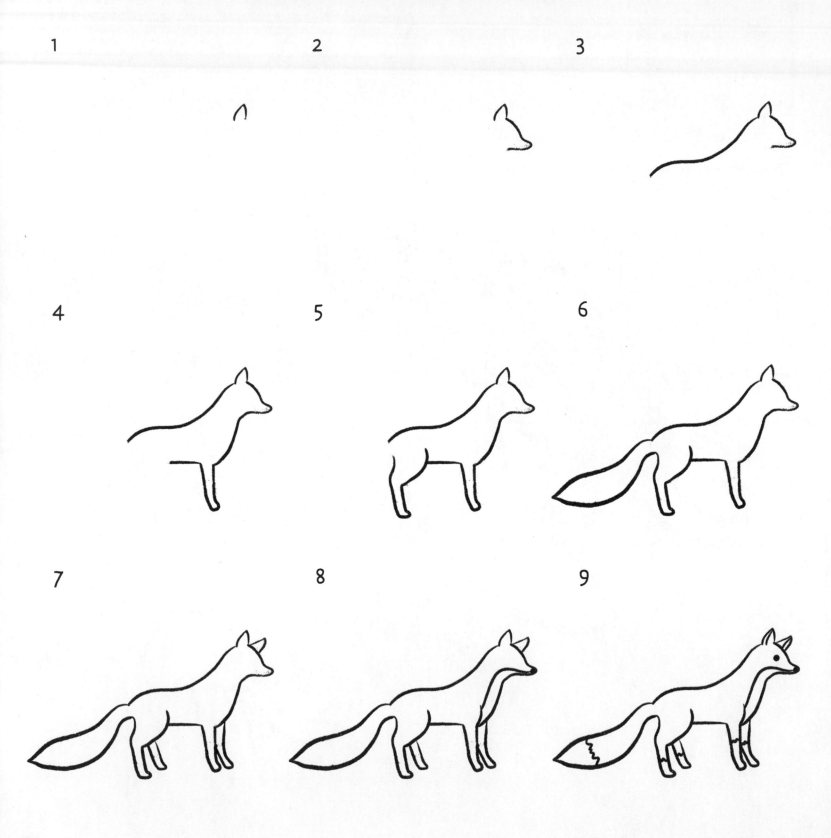

All About Foxes

* Foxes dig dens, or "earths," underground. This is a safe place to raise their babies.

★ Foxes live in most places on Earth, from cities and forests, to deserts and the Arctic.

Let's chat!
Foxes use 28 different calls to communicate with each other.

Clever tails
Foxes use their tails to balance, stay warm, and signal to other foxes.

Turning red
Red foxes like this one are born with brown fur. They turn red when they are a month old.

How to Draw an Elephant

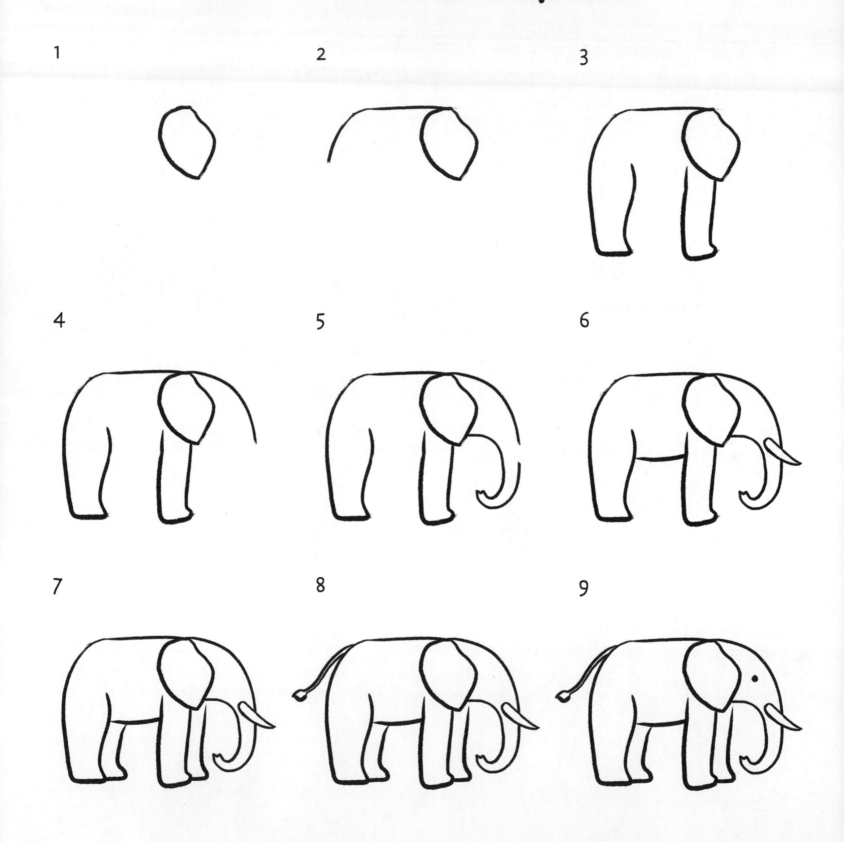

How old?
Elephant tusks never stop growing. The bigger the tusks, the older the elephant!

Wow!
Elephants have 150,000 muscles in their trunks.

All About Elephants

★ African elephants like this grow up to 3 m (9.8 ft) tall and can weigh 7,500 kg (16,500 lb)—the same weight as a small passenger plane!

★ Elephants spend up to 18 hours eating every day.

How to Draw a Beaver

1

2

3

4

5

6

7

8

9

All About Beavers

* Beavers make walls called dams in rivers using sticks, logs, mud, and rocks.

★ They live near the dam, in a home called a lodge.

Warm and dry

Beavers have oily fur that is naturally waterproof.

Tough teeth

Beavers use their strong, sharp teeth to cut down trees, remove bark, and build dams and their homes.

Splish splash

They use their webbed feet and flat tails to swim fast.

93

How to Draw a Panda

1

2

3

4

5

6

7

8

9

★ Baby pandas are pink, hairless, and about the size of a pencil!

Light and dark
Pandas have perfect camouflage: white for snow, black for shady areas.

Not so big ...
Giant pandas are actually just 1.5 m (5 ft) tall. That's shorter than most adult humans!

Hold on!
Instead of thumbs, pandas have extra-long wrist bones to help them grip food.

What an artist! You've learned how to draw animals from all over the world.

Do you know which animals live together in the same places? Try drawing a watering hole with elephants, giraffes, and zebras—or an underwater scene.

Or you could take your animals on a wild adventure. What about drawing a spaceship crewed by squirrels or a submarine full of sloths?

There are no limits when you know how to draw!